Accompanied by two track C.D.
Featuring the famous
and a duet with

Published in the United Kingdom by Philly Books in 2009

OH MEIN PAPA
© Johnny Carroll

First published in paperback in 2009 by Philly Books

Philly Books
18 Bridge Street, Portadown, Co. Armagh, N. Ireland, BT62 1JD
Email: sales@harrisonprint.com

Typeset, Designed and printed by
Harrisons
18 Bridge Street, Portadown, Co. Armagh, N. Ireland, BT62 1JD
Telephone: 0044 (0)28 38 330252
Email: sales@harrisonprint.com

Johnny Carroll
'The Man with the Golden Trumpet'

> *Dedicated to my*
> *loving family*

I wish to thank Philomena Gallagher,
writer and editor, for her encouragement
and support and for providing an
excellent record of my life story.

'OH MEIN PAPA'

Johnny Carroll's own life story
by Philomena Gallagher

**The Galway man
with the Golden Trumpet**

OH MEIN PAPA
© Johnny Carroll

OH MEIN PAPA

© Johnny Carroll

Email: goldentrumpet@iolfree.ie
Telephone: (UK) 00353868511575
(Southern Ireland) 00443868511575

Prologue

Before the days of keyboards electric guitars etc brass instruments dominated the music scene in Ireland and UK. Dance bands were similar to the 'Big Bands' of 1940s or orchestras. They usually had ten to twelve musicians who sat behind music stands while a band leader took centre stage.

Irish people love their music and dancing. There would have been hundreds of ballrooms / parochial halls all over Ireland eg Abbey Hotel in Donegal, Arcadia Ballroom Bray, Tipperary and Cork, Astor Ballroom Belfast, Atlantic Ballroom, Bundoran, Co Donegal, Castle Ballroom, Banbridge NI, Dungiven / Derry, Enniscorthy Co Wexford, Rockhill, Co Donegal, Crystal Ballroom, Dublin too many to mention.

The true era of the Irish Showbands actually started in the 1950's, exploding into every town in Ireland by the 1960's. The term 'Showband' apparently was 'coined' by the Belfast musician Dave Glover. In a Radio interview in

1989 he claimed that although the 'Clipper Carleton' was the first band to put on a show with their regular Saturday night jukebox, he was the first to add the word 'Show' to his band, ie The Dave Glover Showband. Comedy acts, impersonations and other acts would be enjoyed for about an hour and then the dancing would begin.

By the 1960's the brass sound was still very popular. Young men came together for the love of music – to play for 4 – 5 hours for a band fee of about £60! Some bands playing six nights a week. Travelling all over Ireland in rickety old vans, all piled in one on top of the other. By the middle 1960's there would have been at least 800 showbands playing all over Ireland.

The Premier Aces were the pride of Bullintubber Co Roscomon. First known as 'The Pioneer Aces' because none of the band drank alcohol and were all members of the 'Total Abstinence Society'.

The band was put together in part by the late Peter Shanager who had been the leader of 'The Ivy Castle Dance Band' also based in Ballintubber. Peter moved to England and Stephen Treacy and Paddy Malone took control.

The original line up was Paddy Malone (Alto Sax), Andy Malone (Drums), Sonny Ward (Tenor Sax), Stephen Treacy (Accordion), Liam Treacy (Sax, RIP) and Micky Slyman (Vocals & Trombone).

In 1958 they decided to turn professional and expand to an eight piece, adding Frank O'Brien, Co Galway on Hawaiian / Steel Guitar, as well as myself at only thirteen years of age playing trumpet. We made the top ten in Ireland, toured Britain, the USA and Canada. In our heyday in 1966 we attracted 3,300 people to the Casino Ballroom in Castlerea.

Alas, as the turbulent 1960's gave way to the swinging 70's Irish Showbands were beginning to change, specialising in 'pop music'. By early 1980's Ireland's entertainment landscape was changing rapidly into four different themes, pop, country and western, folk and rock music.

The emergence of discos benefited the promoters ie instead of paying a full band they had only to pay one DJ to spin the discs. Ballrooms quickly became 'Night Clubs' and bookings for bands got less and less. By 1980's the showband scene was over. Large audiences of over 2000 and marquees were becoming a memory.

By the late 1990s there has been a renewed interest in dancing again ie: over 50's enjoying Irish Country music. The majority of young people today have never danced to a live band, which is very sad.

The Irish Showband era was an exciting yet hard working time. Many musicians earned a decent wage / living and provided many people with much needed and loved entertainment, while giving the promoters a good living as well.

Dad

Synopsis

Rural Ireland, Castlerea Co. Roscommon in 1951, eight year old Johnny Carroll knew the hardship his parents had in having a shilling to pay for his tin whistle classes and this caused him a lot of stress and concern to please his parents, particularly his Dad.

Joe Carroll, was determined his son would play an instrument and he had a certain sound in his head that he wanted to hear. With great difficulty and determination he achieved his goal when young Johnny at twelve and a half years of age stood in the family's humble kitchen on a Christmas Eve and produced the perfect sound from his new trumpet, bought on Hire Purchase. From thirteen and half years of age Johnny was playing with a successful Irish Showband and contributing to the family's finances.

His Dad's belief in his musical ability enabled him to travel all over the world and to perform with many famous stars. He produced ten albums - five of them Gold albums and is still playing and bringing pleasure into people's lives fifty three years on. There were many hardships and heartaches along the way.

Mum and me aged 6 months

They say God has a plan for all of us and he certainly had the best plan of all when young Rose Caulfield fell in love and married Joseph Carroll.

Both from Castlerea, Co. Roscommon, Ireland, they settled down in Castlerea to build their lives together. Inhabitants of rural Ireland in the 1940's experienced real poverty. There was no electricity, no running water in homes, no access to good employment. People led simple lives, yet they pulled together as a community. Many emigrated to America or England just to earn a living.

Not Joseph, or Joe, Carroll as he was known. A sturdy build of a man with a fiery temper, he was prepared to work at anything so that he could stay and rear his family in his beloved Co. Roscommon.

After two years of married life, in 1945, young Rose presented Joe with a healthy baby boy - small, pale, with a shock of red hair. From the moment Joe held him in his arms there was a bond. I was that boy.

Baptised John Carroll, I was followed some time later by three sisters and one brother. A small two-bedroom house was made comfortable by sheer hard work and a lot of love. My Dad turned his hand to many jobs; labouring on building sites and as a painter at the local Sanatorium in Castlerea. My mother, like all women at that time, kept the house, cooked, cleaned sewed and saw to her husbands and childrens' needs. Life was hard, as it was for everyone at this time, and the Catholic Church played a major role in the lives of this small rural community. People's expectations in life were simple, they were thankful for their lot and, as we would say today, they would not have much to answer for in the next life.'

My Dad was not afraid of hard work and the greatest joy in his life was his music. A small battery radio brought him great pleasure as he listened to Radio Eireann. He never got the chance to play an instrument but God blessed him with a wonderful gift – he was a fine whistler. He could whistle a tune note perfect and throughout his day he would whistle all the old Irish tunes, crystal clear. I, a young fella of five years of age, could only look on in admiration and amazement because no matter how hard I tried, I could not make that sweet sound from my lips.

*Dad, Joe Carroll with my cousin Patsy Haugh
and me on dad's knee*

I was enrolled at the local convent school at five years of age and from that day became known as Johnny Carroll. At eight years of age I was surprised when my Dad enrolled me in a local tin whistle class. Even though times were hard a shilling a week was found for my lessons. This brought extra pressure on me to play well, as I knew from a young age that shillings were hard to come by. As much as I yearned to play a tin whistle I knew my Dad would demand perfection. Only precise, crystal clear notes would be accepted.

Every week I would hurry down to the local hall and join many other young lads for classes; my whole shilling clasped tightly in my hand. Many weeks, embarrassed, I had to apologise to the teacher for not having my shilling and promise faithfully that I would bring two shillings the following week. The teacher always allowed me to stay.

Every day after school I would stand motionless in all weathers, staring into the front window of one of the larger stores in Castlerea because there, lying on a bed of red velvet was the most beautiful tin whistle (penny whistle) I had ever seen. It was long, shiny, black with a gold mouthpiece. How I longed to own that instrument!

In my mind, I held it respectfully to my lips and placed my fingers carefully on the notes and mentally played a melody. I could have stood there for hours, my nose pressed up against the glass. I never told my parents how I longed for that tin whistle, as I knew that even paying for my classes caused much hardship.

Our local boys' band was known as the 'Flaggette Band', and consisted of thirty young boys. Twenty-nine young boys from eight to eleven years of age who could march perfectly and play a march at the same time. Alas, not me! Johnny Carroll could perfectly play the march, but my feet had a rhythm all of their own.

A big parade was planned for Easter Sunday from the local chapel to the cemetery to celebrate the heroes of the 1916 Rising. My Dad was so excited at the prospect of seeing his son in the parade he could hardly enjoy his Sunday lunch. My lunch was doing summersaults in my stomach, at the thought of my dad watching the parade. After the long hard six weeks of Lent, all of the village was eager to enjoy the parade. My Dad made his way to the top of the hill to get a better view as I nervously made my way to the band's meeting place.

◄
*Lookin good at
3 years old*

'Johnny Carroll, will you keep in step!' roared our music teacher, and I did my best, but the tune on my lips produced a different rhythm in my feet and I found myself hauled out of the line.

'You're not going! This parade is not for you!' And I found myself lifted up and set aside. Tears stung the back of my eyes and throat and my heart raced in panic. My lunch made its way half way up my throat and settled there.

'My Dad! My Dad,' my mind shouted.

'He'll kill me,' my brain told me and I started to run towards the hill, stumbling and falling on the way.

The broad back of my Dad faced me. He was busy scanning the parade. Twenty nine young boys all dressed the same. Joe Carroll searching for that familiar shock of red hair.

'Dad' I said meekly. Stunned, he faced me. 'I couldn't play and march, dad,' I managed to stammer out between tears and sobs, 'I'm sorry Dad!' My Dad's face reddened with temper and I paled and stepped backwards. I quickly realised that his temper was directed at the music teacher. 'The bastard! The bloody bastard! He pulled you out. Sure he could have placed you at the back of the parade. It's as well I can't get my hands on him, I'd swing for him. That's it!! You're not going back to his 'Flaggette Band.' And so my tin whistle classes came to an end.

Thankfully, my Dads love of brass band music motivated him even more to have me play an instrument. The 'Castlerea Brass and Reed Band' had been disbanded for many years, so on a Sunday morning at mass when the priest informed everyone that the band was reforming, the air was thick with excitement. It had been a long time since this rural Irish community had a new interest and for many days all I heard was talk of the band.

At this time my Dad was working as a painter and he had a work colleague called Tom McLoughlin who was connected with the band. My dad approached him about me joining the band. 'Any chance of my young fellow joining the band, Tom? Be Jesus, the music is in him but I darn't tell him. I want him to achieve perfection by working hard. He'll not let you down. When he had that

Mum with me aged 3 years old

old tin whistle it was never from his lips Can I bring him down to the hall?'

Aye, bring him down, Joe, though I'm not promising anything. He's very young,' answered Tom. My Dad whistled through his work for the rest of the day.

'Hurry up now and take your tea. We're for the hall. You're going to join the brass band,' my Dad informed me as he slapped me playfully on the back. I had no idea what a brass band was, but eager to please him I leapt on the bar of his old bicycle and off we sped to the local Technical College where classes were to be held.

Castlerea in 1953 consisted of one Church, one cinema, a convent school and the Christian Brothers School which I now attended. 'The Brass and Reed Band' forming again was something to do; somewhere to go, so on the opening night two hundred local people attended. From young boys in their teens to middle aged men, all had gathered in the school, hoping to be selected to play in the band. At 8.30pm my Dad and I were told to go home; there were not enough instruments, and I was too young.

A heavy silence hung between us as we travelled home. Jumping down from the bar of the bike at our front door he caught my small pale face in his rough working class hands and turned me around. Disappointment was etched all over his face. 'Don't you give up, son. If you want it bad enough you fight for it.'

My mother didn't ask any questions. She simply poured two mugs of hot sweet tea and passed them to us. We sat staring into the fire, silent, as the old clock ticked away our lives.

The following week I rode the bicycle myself to the Technical College and sat quietly at the back of the hall listening to every word, drinking in every note and sound. Again I was sent home. I did not give up. A forlorn, small figure in my short trousers, I would sneak in through the back door quietly take my seat, speak not a word and listen intently. Thirty young men had now been selected to play in the band and every week I was sent home and told it was too late for me to be out.

For two months I turned up every week and I noticed that after the sixth week the crowd began to get smaller.

*Myself at four and half
years with sister Rose
Two and half years*

Some boys were losing interest and others perhaps had not the gift they thought they had. You can imagine my amazement when out of the blue one night the bandleader called me from the back of the hall and said to a lad standing beside him, 'Give him an instrument. He has been sitting there for the past two months.' I was handed a tenor horn. I had never seen an instrument like this before and I hadn't a clue how to play it or how it sounded, but nevertheless it was an instrument! My breath came in staccato rhythm as I faced my Dad in the kitchen.

'Dad, Dad, I got an instrument. It's called a tenor horn!' I knew my dad was delighted but he only asked, 'No cornets?' Now to those of you who haven't a clue what a cornet is, let me explain. It is a small trumpet-like instrument that was used in marching bands and 'The Castlerea Brass and Reed Band' had only three, and they had been snatched up. 'I blow and I blow. Dad, but I can't get a sound,' I stammered.

'Keep at it, son, it will come. You're in 'The Castlerea Brass and Reed Band!' and he whistled a happy tune as he stared into the turf fire.

Every Wednesday night I travelled to practise, and within six months I had learned the scales. A fine achievement indeed, as we were not allowed to take the instruments home. Every spare moment I got I practised the scales in my head, pretending to play my tenor horn.

At last 'The Castlerea Brass and Reed Band' was complete. Forty men, boys in their teens; young men from twenty five years of age up and the 'baby' - Johnny Carroll in his short trousers.

My Dad, however, did not give up. Again he confronted a friend, Tom McCormack, who was in the band, to give me a cornet.
'Go on, Tom, give the lad a cornet.' he would urge.

'Jesus, Joe, I haven't got one to give him. There's an old battered cornet must be over twenty five years old lying somewhere. The other cornets are gone.'
'Get it fixed, Tom. How about sending it to Waltons Music Store in Dublin? I heard over the radio they can repair instruments.'
'We'll see, Joe, we'll see!'

*Dad and myself
at 9 years old* ▶

Joe Carroll persisted and within a few weeks I was handed my first cornet. Again the band leader was approached. What the hell do you want now Joe Carroll?' demanded the bandleader.

'I want you to allow Johnny to take the cornet home to practise. I promise you he will take good care of it!' and he offered his hand in a firm handshake.

Every week I would place my cornet into a little bag, tightened at the top, which my mother made for me, and carry it carefully on the handlebars of my bike and cycle home. Every day after school, after my chores, like collecting the water from the well for the familys drinking and washing, I would sit on the edge of my bed and practise my music. This was no chore. I could not wait to get home from school to practise, as I knew my Dad demanded perfection.

My Dad worked all hours to provide for his family. He would only earn about £6 - £7 a week and his one vice was taking a smoke. Often I would watch as he shredded small amounts of turf to resemble tobacco, roll his precious material in paper and smoke contentedly.

Many times my sisters and I longed liked other children to go to the local cinema but money was scarce, very scarce. Sometimes we would only be two pennies short for us to go, so no one went as one would not go without the rest. This loyalty has remained between us today as we all know we are there for one another.

At this time my Dad was caretaker of the local cemetery. This was a job which also offered a house. My Dad talked constantly of me playing a trumpet. I practised hard and often heard him say to my mother;
'Ah Rose, I'd love him to have a trumpet.'

Both my parents were proud of me, as were my siblings, and they always came to watch the band on parade.

I remember going to a local G.A.A. field to play before a big match and always to the cemetery at the Easter Parade. One particular parade sticks out in my mind. The band was to travel to Co.Roscommon to play on a beautiful summers evening. The local butcher had loaned the band his 'bacon van' as a means of transport for the band members. So I was one of the crowd packed like sardines into the unwashed, salty, bacon van. When we escaped some time later to the lush green fields

Woodwork at Castlerea Technical College 1958

where the function was to be held, flies of all sizes, colours and shapes descended on us and ate us alive!!

The older members of the band would get a fee of perhaps £5 for stout and porter to be enjoyed back at the schoolhouse. The band members would stop at John Hunts and minerals (lemonade) would be purchased for the young lads and baby Carroll.

My Dad was seeking a certain sound and he knew it would only be achieved by myself playing a trumpet. While reading his Sunday paper, The Irish Independent, an advertisement caught his eye. Waltons Dublin, Musical Department was offering trumpets for sale.

'Rose, write to them and ask for a catalogue, just to see what is on offer' he instructed my mother, who obediently and quietly obeyed.

Within a week a black and white catalogue arrived in the post. In stunned silence he and I stared at the catalogue. I had never seen so many different types of trumpet. I had no idea what a trumpet sounded like but my Dad knew.

That one!' he said and he pointed to a beautiful silver

Selmer - £27.10 shillings!! A fortune to a man who was only earning £6-£7 a week. But he was determined, and instructed my mother to write off and make arrangements for hire purchase.

My parents had a fear of debt. It was considered a great sin to owe money, yet nearly everything they purchased, especially food and clothes, would have been bought 'on tick', something all the neighbours did too.

It was Christmas 1955. My mother had polished, cooked and cleaned and she and Dad had managed to purchase a few small gifts for our stockings. Our small house swelled with love and faith. A bright turf fire burned in the grate and the old Tilley Lamp had been polished so hard that it shone brightly, offering a comforting glow to the small kitchen in the cold frosty night.

Radio Eireann played Christmas melodies and all of us would join in the Waltons Musical Store's promotion theme: 'If you're going to sing a song; do sing an Irish song'.

Frankie.....had just finished her show on advising a young

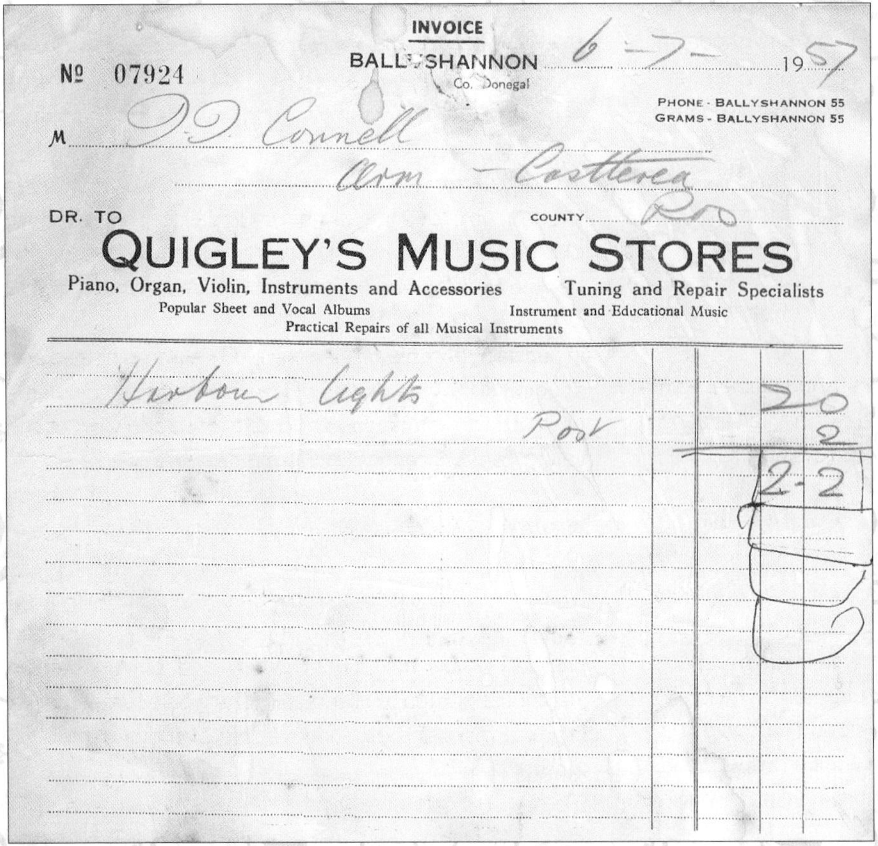

INVOICE

Nº 07924

BALLYSHANNON
Co. Donegal

6 - 7 - 19 57

PHONE - BALLYSHANNON 55
GRAMS - BALLYSHANNON 55

M O'Connell

Arm - Castlerea

DR. TO

COUNTY

QUIGLEY'S MUSIC STORES

Piano, Organ, Violin, Instruments and Accessories   Tuning and Repair Specialists
Popular Sheet and Vocal Albums   Instrument and Educational Music
Practical Repairs of all Musical Instruments

'Harbour Lights'

Post

2 - 0
2

2 - 2

My father would only have earned five shillings a day yet he paid two shillings and two pence postage for the sheet of music to hear 13 year old Johnny play 'Harbour Lights'

farmer on how to ask a local girl to a dance, when the front door was knocked and on opening it I was handed a telegram. Mesmerised, I handed it to my Dad. The small family waited with bated breath; a telegram usually brought bad news.

'It's the trumpet! Rose it has arrived! It's at the station. On your bike, son, and bring your trumpet home!'

My siblings squealed with delight.

'On you go, Johnny! Hurry before the station closes,' and he caught my mother in his arms and twirled her around the small kitchen. This is going to be a fine Christmas, Rose, a fine Christmas indeed!'

Pulling on my coat and scarf, I slipped on the frosty ground as I reached for my bike. Throwing my right leg over the old, battered bike, the frosted cold steel bar nipped tight the skin on the inside of my thigh as my short pants rode high. I rode as fast as I could to the train station. The porter at the station helped me to tie the large cardboard box to the bar of my bike and I cycled home very, very carefully. I was the first in Castlerea to

have a trumpet. Hell! The first in the band to have a trumpet. I had been taught that pride is a sin. At that moment in time I was as proud as a peacock, but with a very nervous young heart beating irregularly in my chest.

The large box was placed on the small, white, wooden kitchen table, and my Dad carefully savoured the cutting and saving of the new string, the lifting off the lid and peeling back the tissue paper and protective covering.

In our dark, humble kitchen the old Tilley lamp hissed and spat out its light begrudgingly, which landed softly on my new, shiny trumpet, causing it to twinkle and wink at the young family present. It illuminated the whole room, causing pale pink, red, blue and purple rays of light to dance a jig around the place.

My parents were speechless. I had never seen anything so beautiful in all my life and my young sisters and brother simply held their breath and stared silently. Time just seemed to stand still. The whole family stared in amazement at the wondrous object before them.

'Go on, son, give us a tune,' pleaded my Dad in a slow

*Lookin even better
and more comfortable
with a trumpet in my hands
aged 13*

quiet voice. I swallowed my underdeveloped Adam's apple and in a high pitched voice could only ask, 'Now?'

'It will take three years to pay for it, son, on hire purchase, so you might as well start now. I'm dying to hear the sound of a trumpet - the first in Castlerea - in my very own kitchen,' and he turned off the radio. My mother smiled and nodded, which really meant, 'Please do as your Dad asks.'

I stepped forward, clenching and unclenching my fists. I had no idea what a trumpet sounded like, so I could only silently pray, 'Dear God, please, oh please do not let me make a mistake!' Lifting the precious object out of the box, which only caused more beautiful coloured rays of light to bounce off the mirror on the wall and the Tilley lamp, I raised it to my lips. My siblings could only take another deep intake of breath at the beautiful sight before settling down to listen to me play.

After practising a few scales I then entertained my dad and family for over half an hour, fearful that my lip would go soft and I would not reach the high notes.
For those of you who do not understand what I mean about the lip, let me explain. To blow and play the trumpet one uses a very small muscle in the lip. This has to be practised every day to give the muscle strength and firmness. If this muscle weakens, the high notes cannot be reached.

'At last, son, at last, we have got the sound I have been looking for. The trumpet is the one for you. Now, all of you, off to bed or you'll get no Christmas presents,' said my Dad as he rubbed his hands together.

I reached for my trumpet.
'No, son, leave it where it is. I just want to sit here and admire it.' and so I left that small, humble kitchen with my trumpet displayed in all its glory as the dancing coloured rays brought a little more magic to a wonderful Christmas.

Every day I would rush home to practise. While other boys kicked ball in the street or chased girls, I blew my trumpet. I was determined to get the sound perfect, determined to get the sound in my head to come out of my lips and into my much treasured possession. After every practise I would clean and polish my trumpet and

A proud father beside his first new car. A Volkswagen Beetle at a cost of £450 bought by Johnny

place it in a small strong canvas bag, tied at the top with string, a bag that my mother had made for me.

Winter give way to Spring and Spring to Summer. When running to the shop for errands the older people would rub my head and say.

'You have a fine sound there, young Carroll. Be Jesus, you'll have them dancing in their graves!'

Or, 'I heard you all the way down the far field. I didn't feel my days work passing, I was enjoying you so much.'
Coming out of Mass on Sundays they would say to my Dad: 'You must be proud of him, Joe. He has come on well. God has blessed him with a wonderful gift.'

I never got to hear my Dad's reply. I would just beam a great big smile at him and my heart would swell with pride at the thought of my Dad being proud of me.

I did not realise that as I sat on my bed playing melodies that they were being carried near and far, up to nearly two miles away, in that quiet calm rural area. It was an era when Castlerea had only one or two cars and the most noise would have been a tractor or a rumbling old bus in the distance.

At this period of time 1956-1957 the music culture was slowly changing in Ireland. A new showband had been formed in Bellturbet Co.Roscommon; a seven piece band known as 'The Premier Aces.' They were travelling all over the country playing at dance halls. One Saturday evening their old van broke down in Castlerea and they were directed to the local garage just across from my house. They were due to play in the Savoy Ballroom on the Sunday night and a big crowd was expected. 'You'll have to leave it, it needs a right bit of repair,' offered Cummins the garage owner. 'Call tomorrow at Joe Carrolls across the road there. He'll have the key to open up.'

'Do you hear that?' asked Paddy Malone, the leader of 'The Premier Aces,' 'Listen,' and the band musicians and the garage owner listened to the clear crystal notes of 'Rose of Tralee' as I sat playing on the edge of my bed, not knowing that I could be heard on that soft, frosty night in March.
'Who is that? Where's that sound coming from?'

The Premier Aces, with Johnny on the far left at 13 years old

demanded Paddy Malone.

'Ah that's Joe Carroll's boy, the young lad over there, that's where you'll get the key tomorrow,' answered Mr Cummins as he pulled shut the garage door. 'That's what we need in our band,' stated Paddy Malone. He says he's very young,' stated another. 'I don't care what age he is, that's the sound we need. I'll have a talk with his dad,' and Paddy Malone did just that.

On the Sunday night at 7.30pm a knock came to our front door. Paddy Malone and two other band members presented themselves. We've come to collect the van,' they said as they stood back and stared up at my bedroom window listening to my playing of 'Shall my Soul Pass through old Ireland?'.

The Premier Aces, seven young men, all Pioneers (they abstained from alcohol) played to a packed house in the Savoy Ballroom as I slept soundly in my bed. Three weeks later Paddy Malone knocked again on my front door and when I opened it he simply asked;

'Would you like to join our band?'
'Me?' I stammered.

Now, earning a wage as a band member had never entered my head, nor my parents' heads. To them my career was all mapped out. Maybe a job at the Post Office delivering telegrams or perhaps as a shop assistant in the local shoe store, earning as much as one pound a week!

'Listen, we're playing a gig tonight. Think it over and we'll call back,' whispered Paddy Malone as he rubbed the top of my head.

'Who was that at the door Johnny?' asked my Dad.

Contributed by John Ryan

Premier Aces Showband

'Dad, they want me to join their band,' I said excitedly. 'Can I dad? Can I join The Premier Aces?' I begged.

'That's not a real band son. You stick with the Brass Band,' and he returned to reading his paper. That was his way of showing me that our conversation was finished.

I looked at my mother, pleading her with my eyes. Placing a finger over her mouth warning me to say nothing, she gave a little smile and winked. 'Please God, I'd love to play with The Premier Aces. Please let Dad let me go,' I begged on bended knees before bed that night.

To my dad, the word showband was not a dirty word, but members of these bands were known to be seasoned drinkers. A crate of Guinness Porter would be on stage with them, and they would consume it throughout the evening. Certainly not fit company for a young naive boy of thirteen and a half years of age.

A week later Paddy Malone knocked again on our door. This time my Dad invited him in. I sat nervously on the stairs straining to hear their conversation. 'We do not drink Sir, we are all Pioneers. We get together for the love of the music,' offered Paddy Malone in a respectful manner. My Dad took a long time to answer. My heart raced in my chest when I heard him reply: 'I'll agree a trial one. He is only thirteen and a half, a few months perhaps.'

'Great,' answered Paddy Malone. 'Now what would you be expecting him to earn? There was a short silence 'I don't know,' said my Dad thoughtfully. 'Just treat him right,' and through the crack in the door I watched as my dad offered Paddy Malone his hand and the two men shook hands as I tried quietly to leave the creaking stairs so that my dad would not know I had been listening.

Every week the band would meet for rehearsals. Paddy Malone would send to Quigleys of Ballyshannon, a music store, for manuscripts of popular music and he would write out my part. It is with thanks to my classes with the 'Brass and Reed band' that I had the knowledge to perfect my music pieces.

Rehearsals would start at 8pm, seven miles away from my home, so with my trumpet in my little canvas bag I would cycle to rehearsals which could go on to eleven

The Premier Aces in New York
Left to right: Jimmy O'Neill (keyboards), Paddy Malone (sax), Billy Ryan (guitar), Houston Wells (vocals), Andy Malone (drums)
Larry Carolan (bass), Johnny Carroll (trumpet) and Sonny Ward (sax).

o' clock. Then Paddy Malone, the band members, me and my bike would be piled up in the old van and driven home. Many times, I was catching up on my homework during the break at rehearsals or when travelling home in the van.

My first real gig was in the Maple Ballroom in Ballinrobe, my first experience of a dance hall. A large silver ball shone down, twinkling and twirling giving the dance hall a magical atmosphere. For one dance, people would be waltzing close together, the next dance they would be jiving mad, twirling the girls so fast that their skirts billowed out showing the tops of stockings, and what I learned later to be suspenders. This was my first time seeing people dance in a half-darkened room and I was soon caught up in the excitement.

I was eager to learn what to do. I did not want to be a burden to the band because of my age. I wanted to 'fit in'. Steven Tracey was our accordion player and after each gig Steven would take out an old 'shammy cloth' and wipe clean his keyboard accordion, no matter how tired he was. He explained to me that after playing in a very smokey hot atmosphere, it was always best to clean your instrument thoroughly to keep it in good order. To this day I clean my trumpet after each gig. I learned from the best.

I had entered a new and exciting, yet fearful, world and my feet could move any way they wanted! No more marching bands for me. Life was magic! The following night we played in the West of Ireland. On the 25th May 1957, Ascension Thursday, I stood in the middle of the line-up with a saxophone player on each side, with large white boards painted with the words 'Premier Aces Showband.' These boards hid everyones legs, so no one could see my short pants.

Two nights work and Paddy Malone handed me thirty shillings (one euro 50 cents in todays money) for each night. I was rich! My dad would have worked all week and would only get £6-£7 pound and here I was with £3! Under Paddy Malone's instructions, I made my way next day to the local shoe shop to purchase a new pair of black leather shoes and I was to get a pair of long trousers.

'Yes, young Carroll, what can I do for you?' asked an abrupt Mr Mangle, the shop's proprietor .'I need a pair of black leather shoes please,' I answered respectfully. 'What do you need black leather shoes for,' he scoffed.

Premiere Aces Showband in 1966
*Left to right: Sonny Ward (sax), Johnny Carroll (trumpet), Larry Carolan (bass), Houston Wells (vocals),
Jimmy O'Neill (guitar/keyboards), Andy Malone (front-drums), Billy Ryan (guitar) and Paddy Malone (sax)*

'I've joined a band, The Premier Aces,' I stated proudly. 'Oh, aye,' grunted Mr Mangle as he wrote my purchase in my family's 'Tick book!' You'll be a long time playing in a band to pay for these shoes. They're thirty shillings,' and he begrudgingly handed me my parcel.

He made me feel so small and intimidated that I quietly met my mother who had bought me my first pair of long trousers.

The following week, I entered the shoe shop and faced Mr Mangle, defiantly. 'Now what can I do for you young Carroll?' he queried in a tiresome voice.'I wish for you to remove the purchase of my shoes from your 'Tick Book.' Here's your thirty shillings Mr Mangle. I got that for playing just one night in the band!' and nodding my head curtly, I bade an open-mouthed Mr Mangle goodbye.

I gave my mother ten shillings and I informed her that a £1 was going into the Post Office every week to pay for my trumpet. Within one year I had cleared the hire purchase on my beloved trumpet and life started to become a little easier for my family now that I at fourteen and a half years of age was working. My musical talent opened many doors for me though I was not aware of this at the time. I loved playing with 'The Premier Aces.' We all got on well together and I recall with fond memory all of the band members.

We travelled all over Ireland to play at various ballrooms for example, Savoy Ballroom, Castlerea; Sea Point Ballroom, Galway; Hanger Ballroom, Galway; Embassy Ballroom, Castleblaney; Gap Ballroom, Omagh; Fairyhouse, Roscommon; Mayflower Ballroom, Drumshambo; Las Vegas in Tipperary; Pavisie in Letterkenny; Butt, Ballybofey, Toreen in Mayo; Roseland in Co. Westmeath; County Hall in Mullingar; Crystal Ballroom in Dublin, Town & Country, Dublin; Arcadia Centre in Arklow and many more.

We played to packed houses - maybe a thousand or more young people - six nights a week, and when dancing was forbidden in Ireland during the six weeks of Lent and the three weeks of Advent [four weeks before Christmas] we travelled to England to play. While in England we played at various ballrooms e.g. Crechism, Holloway Rd. Cricklewood; National in Kilburn and many more wonderful places. Many grand parents today proudly tell their grandchildren that they met and fell in love while dancing to 'The Premier Aces.'

Ballintubber, Co. Roscommon's Premiere Aces
Lineup back row: Andy Malone (drums), Paddy Malone (sax), Jimmy O'Neil (guitar), Frankie O'Brien (guitar) and
Mickey Slyman (trombone). Front: Larry Carolan (bass), Johnny Carroll (trumpet) and Sonny Ward (sax).
The Aces brought in singer Pat McCaul some time later.
The band were original called the Pioneers as they all were (note the pins)!

The journeys to England were a nightmare. I remember my first journey. I was fourteen years old, small and skinny for my age and I had never been on a boat in my life. The boats were called the cattle boats because as well as passengers, hundreds of cattle would be herded on also to travel to England.

I stood at the Dublin docks clutching, like everyone else, a battered brown suitcase held tight with an old belt, and my precious trumpet in the little bag my mother had made for me, and took in the scene.

Up to 800 frightened animals were pushed and shoved on to the bottom deck. Then a crane hoisted up the band's van and swung it over on to the top deck. Finally, we were able to board. I never slept a wink the whole night. There were no comfortable seats or berths. I preferred to sit outside all night on a cold damp seat. If the crossing was a bit rough and it usually was in December, the bellowing of the frightened cattle was deafening and the stench of their opened bowels caught the back of your throat causing the last meal you had eaten to rise fiercely and threaten to escape.

I had never travelled by sea before, so I did not know what to expect. Throughout the entire journey I clung to a slippery hand rail, retching violently; head aching; stomach aching; my legs buckling under me with weakness. All I could do was to pray to God to make the journey end. I honestly thought I was going to die. Others were being sick around me which made the situation worse. I clutched my case tightly in my left hand, fearful I would lose my beloved trumpet with the powerful swell of the sea. It felt as I f the stern of the boat went down, down to the bowels of hell and then rose up again; the whole night long.

The small sheltered area inside was worse. The stench of porter and cigarette and tobacco smoke hung in the air like a thick blue fog. Passengers would be openly sick; fights would break out because of the drink consumed and others would weep openly and loudly about leaving Mother Ireland. Perhaps many of them knew that they would never return home.

It was best to be outside, out of the way. At times like these I missed my sisters, Louise, Rosemary and Martina, my brother Gerry and my parents. The Christmas Eve before, I had received my beautiful new trumpet. Now I sat alone, cold and damp yet excited

The Premier Aces circa 1967
Back left to right: Jimmy O'Neill (keyboards), Bob Madden (guitar), Shay O'Hara (vocals), Sonny Ward (sax), Paddy Malone (sax).
Front: Andy Malone (drums), Johnny Carroll (trumpet), and Larry Carolan (bass).

about playing in England. At 5a.m. at Berkinhead the cattle were taken off first. Two hours later passengers and vehicles prepared to disembark. Our rickety old van with no heating hit the motorways to London, stopping briefly for a chip or a cup of tea. The trips from London to Scotland in bad weather were nightmares. We were chilled to the very bone. To keep warm we would have a fun wrestling match. Every day I worried myself sick about the sea journey home, but telling no one.

I paid attention to all what was going on around me and I can say that I learned the tricks of my trade along the highways and byways of Ireland. I made money, new friends and best of all I got great satisfaction knowing that I was bringing a little financial comfort and security to my parents.

Yes, there are many things a young boy of that age should not have seen, but in hindsight everything was so much more innocent then. 'The Premier Aces,' did not have as many problems as some of the other bands because none of us drank alcohol and we all know the old saying: 'When the drink is in, the wit is out.'

After playing in ballrooms throughout Ireland and England for about three years I purchased a top of the range trumpet from Walton's musical store in Dublin. Only this time, I could walk in and pay cash. No more hire purchase, thank God.

Spring through to autumn was an exciting time in Ireland in the music business. We would travel all over Ireland in an old Zephyr car. The bass drum and other instruments would be tied to the roof rack. Seat belts were unheard of, so three would sit in the front and four would pile into the back. Being the smallest I was always squeezed into the back.

It was not too bad in summer as all the windows would be down, but in bad weather, when six young men would be smoking cigarettes heavily and not realising they were blowing it right into your face, one could feel quite ill after a five or six hour journey. By the time we reached our destination my eyes would be irritated with the smoke and people thought I had been crying for hours.

Easter was a glorious time. After travelling the highways and byways of the UK it was good to be home. The long hard six weeks of Lent were over and the young people were able to meet up again and enjoy the music. Girls would have new dresses for the big Easter Sunday night

The Premier Aces from Roscommon
Left to right: Sonny Ward (sax), Paddy Malone (sax), Johnny Carroll (trumpet), Larry Carolan (bass), Jimmy O'Neill (keyboards), and Houston Wells (vocals). Front: Billy Ryan (guitar) and Andy Malone (drums).

dance and the boys would be dressed in suits, shirts and ties. Many a fine romance began on Easter Sunday night. Marquees were very popular for dances all over Ireland. When we would reach our destination, glad to escape to the fresh air, we would be surrounded by dozens of local children eager to help with our equipment and receive a coloured signed photo of the band.

We always carried a football in the boot of the car. The band would form a team and the kids would select their team and a fine match would be enjoyed. We would kick the life out of that old ball, not realising that it was a wonderful way for us to get rid of our tension and frustrations after such a long journey.

The marquees could hold up to 1500 people and each dance was packed to capacity. There was no such thing as changing rooms. You just went to get changed into the band's uniform outside, at the back of the Marquee. Many a time you would be on your hunkers trying to pull on your trousers when a bus load would pull in, and the yells and whistles were deafening, as they got a good view of your backside.

There was no such thing as toilets. A large tin bucket would have been placed a little way from the Marquee with a cement block to stand on. A sheet of galvanised tin down each side and back, one on the roof, with a sheet of tin to pull across for a door. Toilet paper was unheard of. Nine times out of ten, you would have to walk over cow dung to get to the 'toilet' and if it had been raining, you would be 'gutters to the neck!'

But nobody cared. The young boys and girls accepted the situation and simply got on with enjoying themselves. They were there to dance to the fabulous music and perhaps meet someone who would leave them home on a date and later settle down with. I can't imagine young people accepting such conditions today.

Inside the Marquee, the music would start up and the boys would line up one side with the girls forming a line on the other side. After the first set of dances the boys would get the courage to cross the floor and ask a girl for a dance. Many had more courage than others because they would have consumed alcohol before the dance. Only soft drinks would be available inside the marquee. If a girl turned a boy's request for a dance down he would return to the boys' side of the room to be jeered at by his friends.

Johnny in the 60's,
with the looks of
a star

A large number of girls preferred to stand at the front of the stage, squealing and waving their arms to catch a band members attention. More often than not the boys in the band would be guaranteed a date at the end of the night, a quick court, before travelling the road again. Innocent times compared to today and a true gentleman never kisses and tells!

After gigs we were not allowed to leave the stage until everyone got a chance to get autographs or to speak to the band members. The heat would have been stifling! At times you could actually see 'steam', rising from the large crowd after dancing steadily for over two hours. Your shirt would be sticking to your back and your mouth as dry as a bone.

At one particular gig the organisers apologised for not providing a cup of tea as they had no cups. We searched the place and found old lemonade bottles and washed them out. The tea was made in one big pot, milk and sugar added and then poured into the mineral bottles. We didn't care, it was great to get a drink of tea.

Another time we were travelling home,1962/3 and it was a bitter, bitter cold night with a heavy frost. No heating in the old van. It was so cold the handles of the doors were frosted over. The boys used matches to try and defrost the handles to get the doors open. Once inside we all bundled up, arms folded tight across our chests to try and keep body heat in.

We had travelled several hours when we reached a railway level crossing barrier in Kerry, which was down. It was 4 a.m. and we were blocked from moving forward. The gate house man was tucked up in bed. Our driver blew the horn - no response. He blew it longer and harder - no response. By now the boys were getting irritated because they were exhausted and very, very cold. The horn was blown sharply several times again - no response. Nothing stirred.

'Get out there young Carroll and give them a blast of your trumpet - surely that will waken him', ordered Paddy Malone. The boys moved aside and I squeezed my way to the back door of the van. A freezing blast of cold air hit us as the back doors opened. Swears and prayers could be heard from the boys.

I stood on the frosted ground gulping in the freezing air; teeth chattering in my head; knees knocking together with the cold and a drip on the end of my nose.

Stella

Hurry up Carroll for Jesus sake, wake him up!' shouted one of the boys. I put my trumpet to my lips and started to play "McAlpines Fusiliers". It worked. In no time at all, the gate man's house lit up and he appeared in his pyjamas with an old over coat on, cursing a bucketful at being awakened. By now, half the village had lit up and we were joined by others in their night attire to find out what was happening. The barrier was lifted and we drove on.

'Johnny Carroll, I only meant you to waken the gate keeper, not the whole bloody village' said Paddy Malone and the boys fell about laughing.

Another night we travelled to a gig in Kerry and parked the van in a near by entrance to a field, close to the venue. As we were playing inside we were unaware that it was lashing rain. Four hours later when we returned to the van, it was impossible to get the van out on to the road. It had sunk in the mud. It was now 3 a.m., the venue was closed and one of the boys had to walk in the pitch dark and find a farm house. What seemed like ages later, he returned with the farmer on a tractor, who pulled the van out. A wild wet night in Kerry. We were soaked to the skin, and we had to sit in the van in damp clothes for another couple of hours before we reached home.

Around about 1958/59, we were playing at the Eclipse Ballroom in Ballyhaulis, Co. Mayo, receiving payment of twelve pounds. We were joined on stage by three young men. Brothers Declan, Con Cluskey and John Stokes. They called themselves the 'Harmonichords'. This trio went on to become the famous 'Bachelors' and by the end of 1964 they had scored three top 10's. The first was 'Ramona', followed by 'I wouldn't trade you for the world' and Pat Boone's 1955 hit 'No arms can ever hold you'. On a recent cruise I met them all again and we thoroughly enjoyed reminiscing.

I remember the night Roy Orbinson was on the same bill as 'The Premier Aces'. The venue was packed to the rafters, must have been up to 2000 people present. It was agreed that Roy and his band could use our equipment. The heat in the venue was unbearable. Roy Orbinson came out on stage and started to sing his hit, 'Pretty Woman'. Women were squealing and fainting at the front of the stage. There was pandemonium trying to get these women out. Roy sung another three songs; never said a word to the audience or us waiting back stage. He left the stage and disappeared.

In 1960's a wonderful man called Jimmy McGee hosted the All Stars Gaelic football matches. Jimmy would have

a team of G.A.A. stars of past years and a team made up from show band members. Many a great match was enjoyed in different towns each Monday night. Everyone came to see the match and afterwards there was a dance in the local hall or hotel. Various bands like Joe Dolan and the Drifters, Red Hurley, Dickie Rock, The Royal Blues, etc. could be playing, and one particular evening The Premier Aces, were booked to play.

It was at one of these football matches that I met Stella. Stella was there with her sister and a friend called Donnie Cassidy. I am often asked what attracted me to Stella and I can only answer that she was a real beauty and a lady.

I discovered her name was Stella and she came from Ballymore Co. Westmeath and that she worked as a cashier at Sean Murray's Bar/Restaurant. We got talking during the football match and after the dance I nervously asked her for a date, and was overjoyed when she agreed to meet me.

The Premier Aces did not play on a Monday night so with great excitement I would wash and dress and drive to meet Stella. It was difficult to meet because of the distance but we courted most Monday nights when I was in Ireland and after a three year relationship I finally got the courage and asked her to marry me. We were young and very much in love and we married on 14th February 1968. I was twenty three years old and Stella 19 years old.

We settled down in Castlerea to build a home together. The joy we shared when we discovered Stella was expecting our first child and I experienced sheer delight and pride when I held my first born, my son David, in my arms. David was followed by three wonderful beautiful girls, my daughters Michelle, Priscilla and Zanda.

I was busy travelling all over Ireland to earn a living and Stella was keeping house and seeing to the childrens' needs. I hated travelling to England during Lent and Advent and always longed to get back home to my family. In 1980, Stella and I decided to move house and we looked at many potential homes with excitement. When we first saw Castlemere House in Galway we instantly knew that this was the home for us.

I have many happy memories of the two of us walking through rooms making plans with the children excitedly

The family portrait left to right - David, Michelle, Johnny, Zanda, Stella and Priscilla

arguing over which bedroom would be theirs. We quickly settled in and felt right at home. Our neighbours made us very welcome. Life just seemed to be perfect. I had it all. A career I loved. A beautiful wife and family whom I worshipped. I, Johnny Carroll, was the happiest man alive.

But there is an old saying in Ireland, 'Nobody gets everything in this life' and this was brought sharply home to me when Stella was diagnosed with that frightening horrible word cancer. My Stella, my beautiful Stella at only thirty five years of age, mother of four young children diagnosed with cancer. At first I could not take it in. Cancer was for old people, not a vibrant, fun-loving, young woman.

It was a very difficult time. I had to go to play in the band. That was our livelihood, but I hated leaving her. I would have to stand on stage playing the music and all the time I was wondering how she was. I was constantly praying and hoping my Stella would get better but, alas, the time came when Stella had to stay in Galway hospital. My parents and family were wonderful at this time helping me with the children.

When I would get home from a gig I would go to the hospital as soon as possible. Stella's face would light up when she would see me. I would lift her frail body gently into a wheelchair, make her as comfortable as possible, and wheel her to a place where we could be alone to talk. It was good just to be together to sit in silence, holding hands.

I had spoken with the doctors about Stella's condition but I am sure many of you who have been in the same situation will agree with me – you can't really take it in! You continue to hope and pray against all odds that the doctors have got it wrong.

We both made a pilgrimage to Medjugorie as Stella had a great belief in our blessed lady. We held hands and prayed silently for a miracle - if it was to be God's will. We were praying in the 'Church of Apparation', when I was asked to play my trumpet during the Mass Service.

I hesitated but Stella quietly urged me on. I played several Irish hymns and 'Nearer my God to Thee', the villagers had never heard a trumpet before. That could well have been the last music Stella would have heard me play.

When it comes to entertaining audiences,
Johnny has few peers.

I was constantly praying and hoping my Stella would get better, but after two years of illness, the cancer claimed my beautiful, wonderful wife. At only thirty seven years of age, on a Valentine's day, on our wedding anniversary.

I will have to pay tribute to the marvellous staff at Galway Hospital who took such great care of my Stella. As they lowered my young wife into that hideous wound in Mother Earth, I held my childrens hands and could just not believe that it was happening. I experienced pure physical pain. It was as if there was a knife plunged into my heart and it was being twisted ferociously. Remembering this time now reopens the wound because that dull ache never goes away.

Family and friends rallied round but they all had their own lives to lead. I had to accept that I was a young man in my middle thirties with a family of four to bring up. The eldest was just 14 years old and the baby was only seven years old. There was no such thing as taking sick leave. From I joined the Premier Aces at 13 years you just had to get on with it - even if you were feeling unwell.

Not to play meant there was no wage and the family had to be reared and bills paid. Quite often I would have a cold sore on my lip, no medicines or creams available like today. A dab of after shave or perfume was supposed to help heal it - but it just stung like mad! While playing it would be very painful and the blood would be running into my mouth piece -but the show had to go on!

People often ask how I coped, stating that they could never have managed. But no one can say what they will do until they have to face it.

My family needed me. I would describe it as being on auto pilot. I saw to the children's needs the best I could. There were no social services to help, no counselling or bereavement groups in those days. The children and I had to learn through trial and error. To this day I admire the way women can multi-task. I hadn't a clue! I would ask my eldest daughter how many potatoes Mummy would prepare for dinner - but what child really watches carefully the dinner preparations? Times I got it wrong and boiled enough potatoes for a dozen, other times I hadn't boiled enough.

It is readily recognised today that there are different stages of bereavement - confusion, denial, depression, anger. The children and I were all at different stages.

One child would be weepy for days - weeks, another would refuse to eat, refuse to wash; another would be angry. Our worlds had been thrown into complete turmoil. It was only our strong love as a family and our faith that got us through. Thankfully I had my parents who, though in their retirement years, helped out by minding the children, especially when I had to travel to England. I had to stand up in the band and play the liveliest of tunes as if I hadn't a care in the world and all the time I was heartbroken, frightened and very lonely.

My beautiful children were wonderful and very supportive and to this day I believe my Stella was constantly at my side, in spirit, guiding me. Yes, it was hard, very hard   but thank God I got through it. I would have to play in Donegal or Cork, many miles from home. I would settle the children in after school, see to their evening meal and then set off to play. When I arrived at the destination I would be running about seeking a telephone box that wasn't vandalised (no mobile phones then!) and making sure I always carried enough cash to call home to check in on the kids. My eldest daughter Michelle just fourteen years old would tell me not to worry that they were all O.K. - homeworks completed and all in bed. Always finishing with, 'There is no bread left Daddy,' and I would reassure her that I would be home with fresh bread for breakfast. No matter how far away I was playing, I escaped immediately after the dance and headed home so that I could see the kids off to school, always stopping of at a local bakery to purchase fresh bread.

Coming in quietly about 6.30am 7.00am so as not to awaken them all too early I would find my youngest, who was only seven years old, and missed her mummy so much, sleeping in my bed. When I would ask her what she was doing in my bed she would sleepily whisper, 'Just keeping it warm for you,' and she would lock her two wee arms around my neck and fall back to sleep. My heart was so heavy with grief to know that this lovely little angel missed Stella so much. I could only lie and pray, 'Dear Jesus, please help me get through another day.' and every night I prayed, 'Please help me get through another night.'

Stella's first anniversary was approaching. I was in bits. Those of you who have lost loved ones will know how every anniversary hurts, especially the first one. You

relive every moment. There I was pretending to be coping in front of my kids and my ageing parents when all the time I just wanted to crawl into a dark black hole and block the world out.

I had been offered a gig at Jackson's Hotel in Ballybofey Co. Donegal. I could not bear to be on my own at this time. I needed to be with my children and I knew they needed me, so that they could cope with the anniversary also. I phoned Jacksons and asked if I could bring the children with me and they said yes. When I told the children they were for Donegal, like most kids they were over joyed because they had never stayed in a hotel before. God love them. They were so excited packing their over night bags. We all piled into the car and they chattered and laughed as we went along. I joined in but I could not stop the wonderful memory of my wedding day coupled with the tragedy of Stella's death. I prayed to Stella mentally as I drove along, 'Oh love, help me to keep sane, to cope, grant I don't break down in tears tonight on stage. Be with me. I love you and need you.'

It was the 14th February, Valentine's night - my wedding anniversary and Stella's first anniversary. Up to 1200 – 1500 people were expected at the dance that night. I had just settled the kids into their room when a phone call came through asking me to go to Mr & Mrs Jackson's private house. Curious I made my way. On entering they asked me to sit down and then proceeded to tell me the news that my dad had died.

At seventy two years of age, big Joe Carroll had been in hospital for a couple of weeks, but I never imagined for one minute that I would lose him. What was I to do? How was I going to tell the kids? They adored their grandparents. The Jacksons offered to cancel the function that night; I was more worried about the children. Their Grandad had died on the anniversary of their mother's death. I had taken them to Donegal to try and ease their pain, now I was to add to it.

I asked the Jacksons to give me some time on my own and I went for a walk to try and straighten my thoughts and to grieve privately for my Dad. I walked alone in Ballybofey fighting back a stream of tears, begging God and his most Blessed Holy Mother to release me from the nightmare. As I walked along memories of him came flooding back. The tin whistle. Pushing me to get a trumpet. Even going into debt so I could have one. I knew he was proud of me. Memories of handing him the keys to his own home. He never dreamt he would ever

Johnny being presented with his first album

own his own property, or his son could buy it for him by playing the trumpet. The joy of seeing him sitting behind the wheel of his first new car, I knew he was proud of me. Walking along, lost in my thoughts I begged God, Stella and my Dad to guide me to do the right thing. I sat in a cold dark bus shelter for a while my head in my hands, tears running down my face and somehow I just got a feeling that Stella and dad were urging me on.

I decided I would not spoil the childrens' evening. I would tell them the next day. They would ask why I wasn't playing. I thought of all the people who had bought tickets and were looking forward to their Valentine's evening together. Somehow I just got the feeling that the right thing to do was to play so I returned to the Jacksons and told them not to cancel.

I returned to the hotel room where the children and I knelt down and said the rosary in memory of their mother. Silently to myself I prayed for the dear departed soul of my Dad and prayed for my mother, brother and sisters. No one guessed when I brought my trumpet up to my lips to blow out all the romantic tunes that I really just wanted to curl up and die. I could see people holding hands the way Stella and I had. See them with their arms

around each other, as Stella and I had done, hold each other close as they danced around the hall, as Stella and I had danced and I thought of her, beautiful in her wedding dress and my farewell kiss, never to see her in this life again and when they called for 'Danny Boy,' I just whispered, 'This is for you, Dad.' and played it like I never played it before.

I did not sleep that night. I sat in the chair and watched over my beautiful sleeping children, feeling very much alone, praying to God to help me cope. The following day we had to pass through Knock, so I stopped the car and took the children into the chapel to light a candle for mummy. We all knelt down and said a prayer and it was then I told them that their beloved granddad was with mummy. Our tears flowed. I could only hug them and feel some small comfort with their arms around me.

'The Premier Aces Showband' proved to be so popular that we got invited to travel to the U.S.A. to perform. My travels to U.S.A. provided a different experience to the Irish scene back home. I met a lot of people who had emigrated to places such as New York and Toronto. Here there was an alcohol licence so people could enjoy a drink, the music and the craic which only a room full of

Johnny with the great
Jackie Healey Rae

Irish people can provide. Back home, alcohol was not allowed in dance halls. A few fellows did take a drink before going for a dance, I suppose to get courage to ask a girl for a dance, but once inside the dance hall or marquee, soft drinks only could be purchased.

The American audiences thoroughly enjoyed our music. To them it was a little piece of home. We played City Hall New York two or three times a year, in the 1960's. It was here I met stars like Glen Campbell, Charlie Pride, Andy Williams and other famous people in the music business.

In 1964, we were playing in Manchester where Johnny Cash was playing on his English tour. June Carter was performing also. 'The Carousel Ballroom,' Manchester was packed to the rafters. 'The Premier Aces' were in full swing before Johnny Cash came on stage. He had been listening to us play and as he came on stage with his own band he asked me to play the riff in his very popular hit, Ring of Fire!' I was honoured to join him on stage. He was always one of my idols.

Another idol of mine was the fabulous trumpet player, Eddie Calvert. As soon as I heard Eddie Calvert play the trumpet on my Dad's old radio I knew the trumpet was the instrument for me. Unfortunately I was too young to go to any of his shows when he was playing in Ireland. At thirteen or fourteen years of age I was allowed to play in the band but on my nights off I was not allowed out socially. Eddie Calvert was the first to have a big hit in Europe with, 'Oh Mein Papa.' Other idols of mine were Eddie Fisher, Harry James and Herb Alpert.

By the late 1960's the golden days of the showband scene were fading. The Premier Aces had known twelve to fourteen good years, We were a long time together as a 'family' practically living in each others pockets and like all families our tastes, styles in music were changing. Throughout these years there were good times, the banter and the craic was mighty and there was also the usual personality clashes. Great wonderful years together, but time to move on. So a couple of the band members and myself formed a new country band, known as 'Murphy and The Swallows.' We had a girl singer and things went reasonably well for a while, but work was starting to get scarce. The disco/pop scene was taking over. So I then formed a pop band. I had a lead male singer, called 'Magic,' and as every pop band had a

Magic Mania put on a show to entertain

gimmick our lead singer had a suit that lit up. It was battery operated and this held audiences attention for another while. This Tom Jones image lasted until the mid 70's. It was now getting very expensive to run a band. I had seven musicians to pay and there were transport and management costs. By the 1980's the disco scene was well under way in Ireland. It just seemed that as soon as I got the right front man, singer, drummer, guitarist etc, they would leave and you had to start all over again. It was getting harder and harder to earn a living and I still had a young family to rear.

Times were hard. I remember one Boxing Night. I had a gig in Donegal. The weather was ferocious. I drove from Galway to Donegal in the middle of a storm. Telephone lines were down, trees were strewn across roads. I ran out of diesel and there wasn't a filling station open. I had to call at a farm house and knock the residents up. Thankfully they were able to help me. When I got to Ballyshannon I couldn't get through the town as trees were blocking the road. By the time I got to Creeslough there wasn't a light – all the electricity had been cut off, the venue was closed. I couldn't find a place open to get a cup of tea, so I had to turn the van around and start to make the journey home. There wasn't a dog on the streets - everywhere was closed. I was freezing cold, hungry, tired, so tired I was glad of the 'stop lights' for a chance to rest my eyes, it was lonely and I was praying hard I had enough diesel to get me back home to my family.

I remember I had a gig in Enniscrone and the van's radiator was leaking. The band and I had left Galway early. We had to stop at a farm house in Co. Mayo and get a bucket of water. It seemed every five minutes we had to stop and top up the radiator. The journey home was worse because there was a bad frost. We had to stop at another farm house and get a forty gallon drum of water. We had to take out the back seat to fit this in. The band members took turns topping up the radiator.

Another rainy night in Co. Kerry we skidded of the road and ended up in a field. Thankfully myself and the six band members only suffered mild shock. A passing car gave me a lift into Galway where I was able to contact a mechanic. When we got back to the van, the six lads were huddled together with old newspapers over them to try and keep warm. We were soon back on the road,

Johnny's group had a lead male singer, called Magic, he had a suit that lit up. Audiences loved it!

and after only a few hours sleep we were on our way to another gig. Much credit to the lads who were working with me at this time, for putting up with these conditions- we just looked at this as doing our job!

I was now eight years on my own and my family were growing up and starting to make their own way in the world. I was playing one night at The Devon Hotel, Temple, Galntine, when I got talking to a wonderful lady called Anne Sheenan. The gig was at her brother's hotel and staff had not turned in for work, so Anne was helping out as the receptionist. God does indeed work in mysterious ways because this beautiful person, was to become my life's companion. I had never imagined for one moment that love would once again come into my life. Anne is my rock that I lean on. We married and settled down in Castlemere House, Galway. May God grant us many years together.

With the music scene changing so much I pondered long and hard on what I should do. I had no great education. I wasn't trained to work at anything. All I had was my music, so I came up with the idea of going it alone, going solo! An album of trumpet music! Nobody had ever done this in Ireland before. Phil Coulter on piano, yes, but no

trumpet player had ever done it. Could it be done? A guy from Castlerea - COULD HE DO IT? Why not?

I spoke with my good friend, Donal Cassidy and we both agreed we were going into the unknown. Decisions had to be made. Would I play Irish or American music? Classics? Pop? Country? After much thought, I decided on 'middle of the road' stuff. I was the first musician to do melodies of three and a half or four minutes. My album 'Touch of class' was my first gold album.

Today I now have more control over what I choose for an album than then. The U.S.A. was a different ball game, hence my album 'Songs I love to Play'. The songs on that album were chosen with an American audience in mind. Another good friend of mine, Gerry Quinn, he was a D.J. in Ohio U.S.A and he began playing my album on his Radio Show. He was the first ever to play my music in U.S.A. Soon other D.J's were requesting my album and many emigrants who listened to these Radio Shows were phoning in and requesting my music. I finally got a record deal in the U.S.A. Gerry Quinn helped me with this.

'River Dance' and 'Lord of the Dance' were very popular so the time was right for an album with a Celtic Irish feel.

*Donal Cassidy and former Taoiseach Albert Reynolds
presents Johnny with his first Gold Album*

I soon had concerts in Florida, where I preformed with the great Irish comedian Brendan Grace for about three and a half years. Another good friend of mine, Sandie Gillard, brought my C.D. back to the U.S.A. also, and my popularity grew even more. I had always loved singing but while in 'The Premier Aces' you were given your slot and no one ever asked me to sing. Hence when I decided to be my own front man – it was best for me to sing. To this day when people are purchasing C.D's after my shows I am still amazed at how many ask for the C.D's I am singing on.

At this time I was seriously thinking of living for part of the year in the U.S.A. as this would cut back on the amount of travelling I was doing between U.S.A. and Ireland. By now, I was the only instrumentalist in Ireland with a number one album and would go on to produce seven more very successful albums, four of them became Gold Discs and I had a major hit with 'Oh Mein Papa.'

No matter where I perform 'Oh Mein Papa,' is sure to be requested before the end of the night. This has been my greatest hit. I first heard Eddie Calvert playing it many years ago as I lay in bed listening to the radio and I was instantly attracted to the sound, so much so that I recorded it, never imagining for one second that I would top the pop charts with my interpretation.

I was playing at a venue in Dublin, when a Father Reynolds approached me. He told me a wonderful story . He was connected with 'Boys Town', a popular film which starred Spencer Tracey. He had seen the gig advertised and wanted me to know that one of the young boys constantly played my tape 'A touch of Class'. The boy hadn't a clue who Johnny Carroll was, he just loved the sound of my music. Day and night he would play the tape. It is awesome to think that a child on the other side of the world loving my music.

I thank God constantly for the gift he has given me and delighted to be able to use my gift to bring a little pleasure into so many peoples' lives.

After much consideration on what title to give my story, 'Oh Mein Papa' was very appropriate as it was my biggest hit, and if it wasn't for my Dad encouraging me to learn the trumpet I would not enjoy the life I have today. So my story is also a tribute to my dad - MY Papa.

When I am not playing or entertaining I enjoy reading,

My life's companion, Anne is my rock that I lean on.
We married and settled down in Castlemere House, Galway.

walking, some gardening and being with my family and grandchildren. I have four grandsons, two in Germany and two practically next door. I also enjoy watching old cowboy films and listening to the music of Eddie Fisher, Eddie Calvert, Herb Alpert.

During the troubles in Northern Ireland, especially after The Miami Showband disaster, myself and other musicians did not get the chance to play at venues in the North of Ireland. In all honesty it would have been too risky. So I was delighted when in 2005 Philomena Gallagher, a Community Development Officer for Age Concern N. Ireland, contacted me and asked me to play at a gig in Craigavon, Co. Armagh to celebrate the 60th Anniversary of World War II. To date I play four to five times a year in N. Ireland and am delighted to have received an award from Radio Star listeners for Best Instrumentalist 2007/2008.

The Northern audiences are wonderful. I have made many new friends and fans. Having been denied access to entertainment during the troubles, they know how to enjoy a good nights dancing. And it is thanks to Philomena, a writer and excellent creative writing tutor,

that I completed my life history - my gift to my family, grandchildren and future generations.

From 2004 I have been travelling abroad with a wonderful company known as Enjoy Travel, five to six times a year. Gerry Flynn and I have become firm friends and Enjoy Travel is the only company I know that brings older people together at home and abroad who enjoy Irish country music and Irish dancing. The company is now ten years old and people have enjoyed themselves so much that they keep returning, so that it is now like one big family partying together.

I am happy with travelling abroad as I can do it at my own pace. I can now pick and choose what I want to do and where I want to go. It is now not so much work as a hobby, a pleasure.

People ask how I keep so fit. Well I do not do anything special. I do not have any particular diet. I have a healthy diet, plenty of fruit and vegetables, and I can relax and chill out and enjoy a drink, but I never take alcohol before a show. I have never smoked. In fact I find it very difficult now to sit in a smoky atmosphere. I have always been

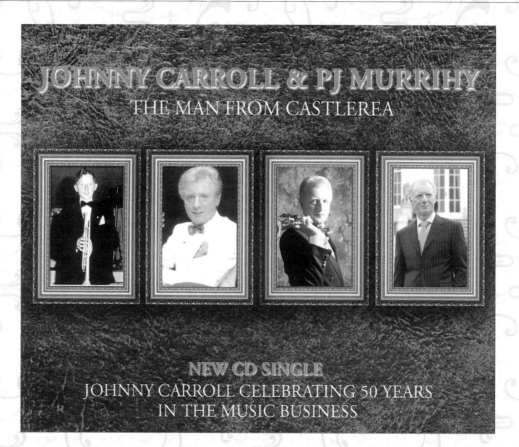

My thanks to my good friend PJ Murrihy

used to hard work. When you have survived the showband days you know no other way. There was no such thing as taking time off for holidays. You just got on with it. Now I can take time to meet my sisters and my brother Gerry. We try to meet up at least four or five times a year. My wonderful mother is now in a nursing home and I get to visit her regularly. Her mobility may have slowed down at ninety four years of age, but thank God her mind is as sharp as a razor. I look forward to and treasure my visits with her.

It has been pointed out to me that I have a little ritual before going on stage. I pause and make the sign of the cross – I bless myself. It is strange how little things like this can become a habit without one knowing it. Well, I always did bless myself before performing, it is my way of asking God to give me the grace to perform well, to give the audience a good show.

People ask me is there anyone I would like to do a duet with, and I readily say yes, with Glen Campbell, one of my idols, and if I have any plans for the future. Well, God willing, I hope to continue working to keep entertaining people as long as I am enjoying it and wanting to do it; to

continue making new friends and meeting old friends, because in the words of George Bernard Shaw:

'Man does not cease to play because he grows old.
  Man grows old, because he ceases to play.'

For me it is not a case of growing old, but getting older and still growing! God willing I will be able to enjoy good health because at the end of the day your health is your wealth.

I have travelled all over the world, performed in many famous places, but the best honour of all was performing at the All Ireland GAA Hurling Finals, at Croke Park. I am a big fan of hurling even though I have never played the game. I was very honoured to represent my country and believe me I was very, very nervous stepping out on to the field in front of thousands of people, and knowing I was being watched by hundreds of thousands of T.V. viewers throughout the world. I have been honoured to play with Artene Boy's Band at four Hurling finals.

In 2008 Anne and I made a pilgrimage to Lourdes in France. I was honoured to play several hymns during the

JOHNNY CARROLL

The West's Awake

1. The West's Awake
2. The Man From Castlerea (featuring P.J. Murrihy)
3. Forty Shades Of Green
4. Lord Of The Dance
5. The Cuilin
6. Country Medley
   Have You Ever Been Lonely
   Ramblin Rose
   Take These Chains From My Heart
   Your Cheatin' Heart
7. How Great Thou Art
8. Nostalgia Medley
   Yellow Bird
   Cherry Pink And Apple Blossom White
   Wheels
9. Irish Medley
   Moonlight In Mayo
   Come Back Paddy Reilly To Ballyjamesduff
   The Mountains Of Mourne
10. Be My Guest
11. Irish Medley
    My Wild Irish Rose
    Boolavogue
    Teddy O'Neill
12. Mise Eire

Executive Producer: Peter Cassidy.
Photography: Dave Cullen.

A CMR Production, 28 Molesworth Street, Dublin 2. Tel: +353 1 6766718. Fax: +353 1 6766482.
Website: www.cmrrecords.ie, E-mail: info@cmrrecords.ie, P & C 2008 CMR Records Ltd.
Special Thanks to: Tom Gilmore, Galway Bay FM, PJ Murrihy, Louis Copeland for supplying Johnny's
wardrobe, The K Club, Straffan, Co. Kildare, Sally O'Brien, Island Ferries, Kylemore Abbey,
Co. Galway, Dan O'Hara's Homestead, Galway, Bernie Brophy's Garden Centre, Tullamore.

PICTURE FORMAT
4:3
COLOUR MODE
COLOUR
REGION CODE
REGION 0
DURATION
56 MIN APPR.
AUDIO CONTENT
STEREO

E
Exempt From
BBFC Classification

CMR RECORDS

5 099141 710140

CMRDVD 1014

DVD
VIDEO

JOHNNY CARROLL

The West's Awake

Featuring the
Hit Single
**The Man
From Castle...**

Filmed on location throughout Ireland

**Featuring: Forty Shades of Green, Lord of the Dance,
Mise Eire, The Mountains of Mourne,
Moonlight in Mayo and Boolavogue**

mass and to pray for the departed souls of my Dad and Stella and all those who have helped me along the way, as I do every day. To this day I still receive ' Memorial Cards' and letters from families telling me that as their loved ones remains were leaving the church my music was played as requested. I feel so humbled and honoured that people love my music so much.

This small guy from Castlerea with his Golden Trumpet made it as a solo artist, 53 years in the music business, and all because of my love for music which helped me provide for my parents and much beloved family – but I could not have done it without you, my sincere loyal friends and fans.

Thank you, and may God bless you all.

Helen &Michael Flaherty (Clifden)
Streatham
London SW16 6BW

Dear Johnny

It was such a pleasure seeing and hearing you play again this year in Ibiza, you honestly get better every year and it's always a real pleasure to talk to you. Your CD playing I'll Silencio (not sure about the spelling!) behind the fireworks display and your final performance in the main Ballroom would be very hard acts to top anywhere! We have also had the greatest of pleasure from listening to your CD's over and over in our own lounge.

You are without doubt and not trying to give you a big head, as if, one of the finest Trumpeters we have ever heard, and the wonderful diversity of the range of music that you play underlines this! I couldn't resist writing you a small tribute to qualify what I'm saying. Hope you don't mind!

You might see Martin Conroy in Portugal!

Much respect and kindest regards

The Fantastic Johnny Carroll

What a gentleman, what a talent, what a performer
He makes music that resounds in your ears
It takes you to somewhere close to heaven
Yet it can also reduce you, to beautiful tears.

That Golden Trumpet gleamed as he played
And filled the heavenly choirs full of cheer
As they listened to the magic of Johnny Carroll
Performing in Ibiza this year.

This amazing entertainer cannot be described
You just have to experience him play
And then be drawn into a new dimension
As he blows that Golden Trumpet, in his own inimitable way.

Then as he lowers the horn, that voice emerges
And almost takes your breath away
A throaty delivery, filled with expression
That you could listen to night and day.

Surrounded by palm trees and a deep blue ocean
Johnny reached out to everyone
This ultimate professional, loving his audience
Creating an atmosphere second to none.

While Herb Alpert, Eddie Calvert and a host of others
Played great melodies during their musical session's
The great Johnny Carroll is melodically superior
As he performs all his shows, with his own special passion.

On Saturday night, as we watched a fantastic display of fireworks
Suddenly, Johnny Carroll's haunting I'll Silencio filled the midnight air
While hundreds of revellers listened in awed silence
Everyone knew, they had witnessed something rare.

As Johnny Carroll played the last strains of I'll Silencio
The watching crowd were touched to the core
Most were feeling deeply emotional
As they listened to Johnny's delivery, of that awe-inspiring score.

Dressed to titillate the discerning eye
Presenting an image that we've loved at every show
Providing his audience with simple perfection
As those who've witnessed, his performances will know.

Just listening to Johnny Carroll's music each night
Was like being raised, on angels wings in flight
With his tapestry of musical renditions
Filling dancers, and listeners with delight.

Large in talent, hugely professional
Each presentation full of "Joy de Vie"
An Irish entertainer who is still as fresh
As when he began that forty six year career, originally.

As he ended his final session with a flourish
He left an aching stillness in the Ballroom air
Then the audience clapped, shouted and cheered
Not wishing this magic to end there.

As they clapped and whistled they shouted encore
Screaming for more and more
Behind him Seamus Shannon played a mean Trombone
While Mary O'Brien and the Enjoy Travel band, were out on their own.

He nodded to Seamus and then to the band
And they did an up-tempo version of Alexander's Ragtime Band
His deep throaty voice punched the words into the air
In a resounding rendition that made the dancers stop and stare.

A harmony of singing, blending instruments with his voice
As Gerry Flynn played the drums with great flair
Then a final burst of magic from that Golden Trumpet
Brought an end, to our wonderful festivities there.

A strong family man with a deep caring heart
Was our Star performer this year
This gentle, caring, unassuming individual
Made us sing, dance, thrill with delight, and also at times weep a tear!

Premier Aces 25 year re-union. They havn't changed a bit ! ! !

What a Show! Johnny performs and gets up close with his audience in Craigavon

Writer / Editor - Philomena Gallagher

I first met J.C. at Lisdoonvarna in 1998. It was a bright sunny Sunday midday when my sister and I entered a large hotel to find hundreds of people dancing to J.C. and his band.

I had never heard of J.C. as my dancing days began at the end of the showband scene, but I was a big fan of the trumpet player Herb Alpert. My sister was a fan of J.C. though she had never seen him perform live. She had only heard him over RTE Radio, Wow! I was blown away, J.C. was fantastic!

My sister said she would love his autograph and a photograph taken with him but she would not ask. Considering myself an assertive woman, I pushed my way through the vast crowd and finally got talking to Johnny and highlighted my sister's request, pointing to her sitting at the back of the room.

Johnny agreed to meet with us after the show, which continued to last for over an hour. I honestly thought he would forget as there were so many talking to him, but he didn't. When the dance ended and the crowd lessened, though exhausted, he made his way to our table, chatted with us and posed for photographs.

We informed him that we were delighted to hear that he was performing again at the same venue that evening. The show was to begin again at eight o clock, by now it was only six thirty. Johnny highlighted that to leave and return we would have to pay £10 each admission and that if we wished he would go and get us some sandwiches. This great star, was prepared to go out of his way to see to our needs! We thanked him of course and assured him we would enjoy a liquid refreshment, and his fabulous show.

I am a great believer in what goes around comes around, and seven years later 2005, through my work as a COMM. DEV. OFFICER for Age Concern N.Ireland I returned his kindness.

I was organising a celebration event to celebrate the 60th Anniversary of World War II. Over three hundred over-fifties were to attend. During those seven years I had spoken with older peoples' groups and discovered that there were many, many fans of Johnny who had only heard him over the radio and indeed had great difficulty purchasing tapes or C.D's.

Well, I needed the best to entertain at a reminiscence W.W.II. dance and to play 'The Last Post,' in honour of all those who had lost their lives during the war, and I felt that the older people who had lived through The Troubles, deserved to hear and meet their idol, so I contacted Johnny Carroll.

An absolutely marvellous evening was provided by Johnny Carroll and Breakaway, and there wasn't a dry eye in the house after Johnny's rendering of 'The Last Post'.

Johnny is a born perfectionist who delivers a professional performance every time, It doesn't matter if he is playing to a small audience or to hundreds. He is an outstanding musician whose unique brand of music gives pleasure to thousands of people. Johnny is Irelands most successful trumpet player and is well known, loved, admired and respected throughout Ireland, UK, Europe, USA and Canada. From 2005 Johnny has played in the North four to five times a year, mostly in County Armagh & County Down, but there are many other fans waiting to see him perform live.

As a writer I was fascinated with Johnny's life story which I usually heard in dribs and drabs while he was having a meal. Johnny usually travels all the way from Galway, gives a marvellous performance and then makes the long journey home. I suggested he should publish his story and was delighted when he asked me to work with him as writer and editor.

I am honoured and privileged to have the chance to write his story. It is an absolute pleasure as Johnny is a born story teller. I hope I have written it well, done him proud and helped him to leave a fabulous record of his life for his family, future generations and his many loyal, sincere friends and fans.

Regards
Philomena Gallagher
Email: philomena1.gallagher@googlemail.com

Family Photo Album

Holiday 2008

The Galway man
with the Golden Trumpet

A day by the sea with Granda Johnny

Baby Evan,
Johnny, Anne
and Family

My grandsons
Philip and Robin
who live in Germany

Evan and baby Alex

*Evan on his first day
at school with baby Alex
and Mum Michelle*

Johnny and grandson Evan 'Hitting the high notes'
© Photo by John Carlos

Evan and Alex getting Music lessons with Granda Johnny

Johnny and Anne with son David and his sisters

Anne and Johnny - Tunisia 2007

New Zealand - 2008

Watch and learn - Show me that note again

Quality time with my beautiful daughters Zanda, Michele and Priscilla

My son David with his sisters

Anne and Johnny Christmas 2005

Daddys' Girls

Mum, still my number one fan.
94 years of age

One of my many appearances on R.T.E. Television

*The following pages are a
brief written history of the Premier Aces*

Story by kind permission of John Baird and Gerry Gallagher

Pioneer Aces - Ballintubber, Co. Roscommon - 1958
The Pioneer Aces (note their pioneer pins) were so named because every member of the band was a Pioneer (no alcoholic beverages).
Back row Left to right: Paddy Malone (sax), Andy Malone (drums), Mickey Slyman (trombone), Sonny Ward (sax),
Front row Left to Right: Liam Treacy (sax), Johnny Carroll (trumpet), Stephen Treacy (accordion),

The Premier Aces

Story by John Baird and Gerry Gallagher

The pride of Ballintubber, Co. Roscommon, The Premier Aces started their careers known as The Pioneer Aces as none of the band drank alcohol and all were members of The Total Abstinence Society. The band was put together, in part, by the late Peter Shanagher, who had been the leader of the Ivy Caste Dance Band, also based in Ballintubber. However, Peter emigrated to England in 1956 before the band hit the road and handed over the reins to Stephen Treacy and Paddy Malone. The original line up was: Paddy Malone (alto sax), Andy Malone (drums), Sonny Ward (tenor sax), Stephen Treacy (accordion) Liam Treacy (RIP-sax) and Mickey Slyman (vocals and trombone).

In 1958, the band decided to turn pro and expanded to an eight piece adding Co. Galway man Frank O'Brien on Hawaiian/Steel Guitar as well as a very young (13 year old) trumpet player, Johnny Carroll (the same Johnny Carroll that is so popular in cabaret these days).

The showband started to command quite a following on the regional scene and the bookings rolled in. However, after several years a dispute with the society forced them to change their name, so they became The Premier Aces around 1959.

Around this time, the Treacy brothers (Stephen and Liam) decided to form their own band, The Rhythm Stars (also from Ballintubber) with three of their brothers, Aidan, Al and Sylvester, this made them somewhat unique on the showband scene at the time....five brothers in the same band at the same time.

At this point, the band added Larry Carolan on bass, and Jimmy O'Neill (brother of Glenamaddy's Joe O'Neill) on guitar. Jimmy would eventually switch over to keyboards.

The Premier Aces circa early 1965

Back left to right:
Michael Slyman (trombone),
Billy Ryan (guitar),
Jimmy O'Neill (keyboards),
Johnny Carroll (trumpet),
Sonny Ward (sax)
Andy Malone (back-drums)
and Paddy Malone (sax).
Front: Larry Carolan (bass).

The band would undergo another change when Frank O'Brien was replaced on guitar by Cork man, Billy Ryan.

While playing the usual Lenten trips to the UK, they came to the attention of an English Country singer, Houston Wells who was fronting his own band, The Marksmen. Houston, born as Andy Smith in Northumberland had a varied career and was once a lumberjack in Canada before becoming a singer. He would fit in straight away with the band and was very popular in the ballroom and marquee circuit as were the Premiers.

Now a nine piece, the band enjoyed new success across Ireland and had a number of Irish chart entries with Above and Beyond, When my Blue Moon turns to Gold, and Only the Heartaches. The band went from strength to strength, becoming one of the top bands in the West of Ireland. Shortly after Houston joined, long time member Michael Slyman called it quits and the band reverted to an eight piece for the next few years. Although Houston's tenure with the band wasn't long

(around a year), his impact on their popularity was immense. In late 1966, the band toured the United States and continued to draw large crowds in Ireland.

In April 1968, a major change took place in the band when Houston Wells was replaced by former Royal Blues singer Shay O'Hara. At loose ends, Houston talked of forming his own band in an April interview in Spotlight, but ended up returning to England where he formed a group called The Masters. After recording a couple of records with them, he would eventually return to Ireland to join The Trident Showband from Limerick. Meanwhile Shay O'Hara, an excellent vocalist with a large following in the West of Ireland, recorded a single with the Premier Aces, the A side entitled Your Lily White Hands. Another change took place when Billy Ryan left and was replaced by guitarist, Bob Madden.

As the sixties came to close, the Premiers had undergone several changes, but were still at the top of their form, a 1969 Spotlight Poll ranked them as one of

Swallows Showband

the top twenty showbands in the country in the same company with bands like the Capitol Showband. Yet, after a very successful run on the showband scene, over which they gave dancers and fans great entertainment, they played their last date at the Oranmore Carnival, Co. Galway in 1969. The band did come together for a time in 1970, but it was short-lived.

However, in 1972, several ex-members of the Rhythm Stars formed a new version of The Premier Aces with local singer, Patsy McCaul out front. The lineup included Aidan, Sylvie and Al Treacy (brothers of original Pioneer Aces, Liam (RIP) and Stephen). Also in the lineup were Dene Lane and Johnny Staunton. None of the band members had even been in the Premiers Aces themselves though. By 1974, both the New Premiers and the Rhythm Stars were history and Patsy McCaul went on to form a country band, Southbound. Since then, the Premier Aces have reunited a few times one of them being at a special dance in the Seapoint Ballroom, Galway just a few years ago.

Following the Premier's breakup in 1969, Sonny Ward, Jimmy O'Neil, and Johnny Carroll formed a country outfit, The Swallows, in 1970 which enjoyed some success early in the 1970's. By 1974 though, Jimmy and Johnny were on the move again and they formed Magic and the Magic Band with only Johnny Carroll and drummer Mickey Belton coming from the Swallows. The new band was originally Magic and the Swallows but soon became The Magic Band. Magic broke up in the early 80's, but Johnny Carroll went on to a solo career known as Ireland's "Man with the Golden Trumpet."

Story by John Baird and Gerry Gallagher
(Thanks to Eddie Kelly for his assistance with some details in this article.)

For more information about the Irish Showband scene, log on to - www.irishshowbands.com

English Country singer
Houston Wells

A pictorial journey through Johnny's life and achievements

Photo by: Nancy McEntee

Ireland's "Golden Trumpeter"
Johnny performs at the
7th Annual Ohio Irish Festival

1988 All Ireland Hurling Final at Croke Park. Johnny was the first ever to play with Artene Boys Band, he played a further four times with the the band at Hurling Finals.

115

PRESS RELEASE

Johnny Carroll Signs Worldwide Deal with Harmac Music

Galway artist JOHNNY CARROLL has just signed a major recording contract with Ireland's newest and most successful TV Marketing Recording Company HARMAC MUSIC.

The first album on the label called "A Touch of Class" was launched last week at a reception in Dublin. The album features twenty tracks of trumpet and instrumental classics with the man with the Golden Trumpet in superb form.

It was produced by Eamonn Campbell with the backing of Ireland's leading session musicians, and recorded over a two month period in Windmill and Westland Studios, Dublin.

Harmac intend utilizing their marketing and promotional skills in promoting the album and start advertising on both radio and T.V. immediately.

It is intended that "A Touch of Class" will be released shortly in Canada, USA, Australia and New Zealand.

A treasured signed photograph from Glenn Campbell

Showaddywaddy Band.

Andy Williams

Johnny with BB,
RTE Television
fame and friend
Mrs. Ann Lenilon

Sandie Gillard Glen Campbell's
Photographer and Johnny's agent in USA

*Home coming of the victorious
Galway Hurling team
with captain Conor Hayes*

Johnny's first video, presented by Maria Geoghan Quinn

Anne and Johnny on holiday with Brendan Bowyer (Huckle Buck fame)

In 2008 Anne and I made a pilgrimage to Lourds in France. I was honoured to play several times during Mass.

Premier Aces Showband
The Premier Aces were (left to right): Andy Malone (drums), Sonny Ward (sax), Larry Carolan (bass), Jimmy O'Neill (keyboards),
Johnny Carroll (trumpet), Paddy Malone (sax), Billy Ryan (guitar) and Houston Wells (vocals-seated).

Glen Campbell

Charlie Pride

Donal Cassidy

*Brendan Bowyer
and myself
relaxing on holiday*

PREMIER ACES SHOWBAND

BALLINTUBBER, CO. ROSCOMMON

Phone 10

JANUARY 1964

Sun	Mon	Tue	Wed	Thu	Fri	Sat
			1	2	3	4
5	6	7	8	9	10	11
12	13	14	15	16	17	18
19	20	21	22	23	24	25
26	27	28	29	30	31	

May Donnelly from Armagh, a loyal fan for many years, kept this Premier Aces calendar safe and sound

Johnnys Albums

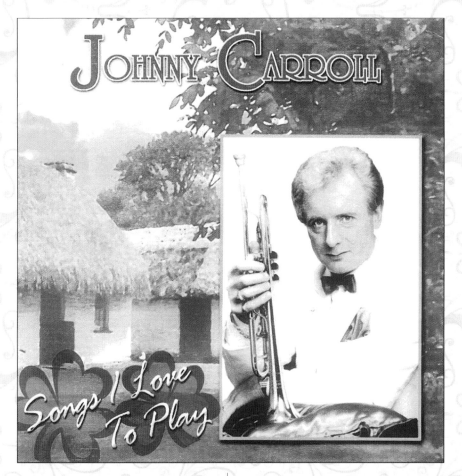

Sounds of Ireland

1. Forty Shades of Green
2. Bright Silvery Light of the Moon
3. Maggie
4. I'll Take You Home Again Kathleen
5. Danny Boy
6. Slievenamon • • The Moon Behind the Hill • The Isle of Innisfree
7. Mary From Dungloe
8. If We Only Had Old Ireland Over Here
9. The Old Rugged Cross
10. The Spinning Wheel • Grace • Rose of Mooncoin
11. The Old Rustic Bridge By The Mill
12. The Rose of Allendale
13. The Old Bog Road • Green Glens of Antrim • Noreen Bawn
14. Whispering Hope

Sounds of Ireland
20 Beautiful Instrumental Airs and Melodies of Ireland
Featuring Johnny Carroll

• Forty Shades Of Green • Maggie • Danny Boy
• Rose Of Allendale • Mary From Dungloe
• I'll Take You Home Again Kathleen

Johnny Carroll's Christmas Favourites

1. SILENT NIGHT
(Trad. Arr. Cassidy/Carroll) Asdee Music
2. O HOLY NIGHT
(Trad. Arr. Cassidy/Carroll) Asdee Music
3. WHEN A CHILD IS BORN
(Zacar/Jay) Siae/Ardmore & Beechwood Music
4. ANY DREAM WILL DO
(Webber/Rice) Webber/Rice/Novello & Co. Ltd.
5. WHITE CHRISTMAS
(Berlin) Irving Berlin
6. MEDLEY : O LITTLE TOWN OF
BETHLEHEM/MARY'S BOY CHILD
(Trad. Arr. Cassidy/Carroll) Asdee Music
I SAW MAMMY KISSING SANTA CLAUS
(Connor)   Blue Ribbon Music
7. OH COME ALL YE FAITHFUL
(Trad. Arr. Cassidy/Carroll) Asdee Music
8. AWAY IN A MANGER
(Trad.Arr. Cassidy/Carroll) Asdee Music
9. THE CHRISTMAS SONG
(Trad. Arr. Cassidy/Carroll) Asdee Music
10. MEDLEY : JOY TO THE WORLD
DECK THE HALLS, JINGLE BELLS
(Trad. Arr. Cassidy/Carroll) Asdee Music
11. ONCE IN ROYAL DAVID CITY
(Trad. Arr. Cassidy/Carroll) Asdee Music
12. PEACE ON EARTH
(Trad. Arr. Cassidy/Carroll)

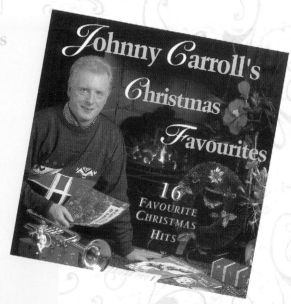

Johnny Carroll's Christmas Favourites
16 FAVOURITE CHRISTMAS HITS

JOHNNY CARROLL

BE MY GUEST

FEATURING

WHITE ROSE OF ATHENS
MY WILD IRISH ROSE
HOW GREAT THOU ART
SAIL ALONG SILVERY MOON
BLUEBERRY HILL
THE ROSE

AND MANY MORE...

SPECIAL GUEST ARTIST - JACKIE HEALY RAE

TRUMPET / VOCALS	JOHNNY CARROLL
SAXOPHONE	JACKIE HEALY RAE
DRUMS	DECLAN O'DONOGHUE
HARMONY	LORRAINE MCDONNELL
STRING ARR.	CARL HESSION
VIOLIN	PATRICIA GLESSON
VIOLIN	ANN MARIE TAYLOR
VIOLIN	YVETTE MOORCROFT
CELLO	CARMEL KELLY
STEEL	GERALD O'DONOGHUE
GUITAR/ACC/BASS.	FRANKIE COLOHAN
HARMONY/MANDOLIN	

BE MY GUEST 1
WHITE ROSE OF ATHENS 2
BLUEBERRY HILL 3
SAIL ALONG SILVERY MOON
MY HEART WILL GO ON 4
(LOVE THEME "TITANIC")
MEDLEY 5
- YELLOW BIRD
- CHERRY PINK AND APPLE BLOSSOM WHITE
- WHEELS
ONLY MAKE BELIEVE 6
IRISH MEDLEY 7
- MY WILD IRISH ROSE
- BOOLAVOGUE
- TEDDY O'NEILL
TIJUANA TAXI 8
HOW GREAT THOU ART 9
COUNTRY MEDLEY 10
- SEND ME THE PILLOW YOU DREAM ON
- BLACK HILLS OF DAKOTA
- BACK HOME AGAIN
WHISTLING RUFUS 11
MEDLEY 12
- THERE GOES MY EVERYTHING
- LAST WALTZ
- ALMOST PERSUADED
BLUE MOON OF KENTUCKY 13
THE ROSE 14

134

From the Heart
Johnny Carroll

1. **COUNTRY BLUES** (4.01)
R. Denova – Quatermass Music

2. **GOLDEN MEDLEY** (4.40)
(A) Tennessee Waltz
Cassidy/Hurley – Asdee Music
(B) He'll Have To Go
J & A Allison – Campbell/Connolly Music
(C) From The Candy Store on the Corner
Hillard – Cop Con

3. **THE LOVELIEST NIGHT OF THE YEAR**
(3.00)
Webster – Cop Con

4. **BLUE EYES CRYING IN THE RAIN** (2.44)
F. Rose – Campbell/Connolly Music

5. **COUNTIES MEDLEY** (3.00)
(A) The Boys From The County Mayo
Cassidy/Hurley – Asdee Music
(B) The Boys From The County Armagh
Cassidy/Hurley – Asdee Music
(C) Lovely Leitrim
P. Fitzpatrick – R & B Music

6. **THE WEDDING SONG** (3.50)
F. Jay/Prieto – Peter Maurice Music

7. **CELEBRATION MEDLEY** (3.28)
(A) Congratulations
Coulter/Martin – Peter Maurice Music
(B) For He's A Jolly Good Fellow
Cassidy/Hurley – Asdee Music
(C) Auld Land Syne
Cassidy/Hurley – Asdee Music

8. **MARY FROM DUNLOE** (2.58)
Cassidy/Hurley – Asdee Music

9. **HITS MEDLEY** (6.30)
(A) South of the Border
Kennedy/Carr – Peter Maurice Music
(B) Red Sails in the Sunset
Kennedy/Grosz
– Peter Maurice Music/Redwood Music
(C) The Three Bells (Jimmy Brown Song)
SDRM/J. Villard – Southern Music
(D) Have I Told You Lately That I Love You
Wiseman – MCA Music

10. **ISLE OF CAPRI** (2.40)
Kennedy/Grosz – Peter Maurice/Redwood Music

11. **THE WALTZ MEDLEY** (3.58)
(A) The Old Bog Road
O'Farrelly/Brayton – Manuscript
(B) The Green Glens of Antrim
Cassidy/Hurley – Asdee Music
(C) Noreen Bawn
Cassidy/Hurley – Asdee Music

12. **EDELWEISS** (2.26)
Rogers/Hammerstein – EMI Music

DESIGN: CREATIVE A.D.

ARTIST MANAGEMENT 091-25542
CMR RECORDS, 5 LOMBARD STREET, DUBLIN 2.

1. THE HAPPY DAYS MEDLEY
You Are My Sunshine, Down By The Riverside, Bill Bailey (Won't You Please Come Home),
Don't Sit Under The Apple Tree, Tavern In The Town, Red Red Robin,
Happy Days Are Here Again, When The Saints Go Marching In.

2. HARRY BELAFONTE
Island In The Sun, The Banana Boat Song, Jamaican Farewell.

3. ELVIS PRESLEY
The Wonder of You , Good Luck Charm, Can't Help Falling In Love With You

4. FOSTER & ALLEN
Moonlight in Mayo, Come Back Paddy Reilly to Ballyjamesduff, The Mountains of Mourne

5. JIM REEVES
Moonlight & Roses, Distant Drums, I Love You Because

6. VERA LYNN
Lili Marlene, We'll Meet Again, Yours

7. NEIL DIAMOND
Song Sung Blue, Cracklin' Rosie, Sweet Caroline

8. WHISPERING HOPE

9. JOE DOLAN
I Love You More and More Everyday , My Own Peculiar Way, The Answer to Everything

10. BING CROSBY
When Irish Eyes Are Smiling, How Can You Buy Killarney, Too-Ra-Loo-Ra Loo-Ra
(An Irish Lullaby)

11. NAT KING COLE
Unforgettable, Mona Lisa, When I Fall In Love

12. RUBY MURRAY
Now Is The Hour, When I Grow Too Old To Dream

Legends
Johnny Carroll

JOHNNY CARROLL
& FRIENDS

Featuring:

PADDY COLE, BRENDAN GRACE, FOSTER & ALLEN, ISLA GRANT,

DESSIE O'HALLORAN, HUGO DUNCAN, AL GRANT, P.J. MURRIHY,

SEAMUS SHANNON & PRISCILLA CARROLL

1. **Be My Life's Companion** (3:18)
(Malton Delugg, Bob Hilliard) Amy Dee Music Corp.

2. **Galway Bay Selections** (3:54)
'Galway Bay' (Colohan)
McCullough/Piggon/Colohan
'Fields of Athenry' (Pete St John) Celtic Songs
'Connemara Cradle Song'
(Murphy)Waltons/Box/Cox*

3. **In Laguna** (3:05)
(G. H. Russell, R. Evans & J. Livingston)
By George Publishing

4. **Orange Color Sky** (2:21)
(M. Delugg, W. Stein) Amy Dee Music Corp.

5. **Poor Man's Roses** (2:33)
(M. Delugg, B. Hilliard)
Amy Dee Music Corp./Better Half-Born Music

6. **The Cuilin** (3:35)
(Maher/Colohan/Cassidy Traditional Arr.)
Assdee Music*

7. **Brahms Lullaby** (2:51)
(Brahms) Asdee Music*

8. **Whispering Hope** (4:08)
(Traditional Arr. Maher/Cassidy) Asdee Music*

9. **Spanish Eyes** (2:45)
(Kaempfert/Singleton/Snyder)
Campbell/Connolly Music*

10. **I'll Walk With the Rain** (2:48) *(G. H.*
Russell) By George Publishing ASCAP

11. **Blue Eyes Crying in the Rain** (2:42)
(F. Rose) Campbell/Connolly Music*

12. **IL Silenzio** (2:59)
(Cop.Con.) MCPS*

13. **My Heart Will Go On** (4:32)
ILove Theme From The Titanic (Horner/Jennings)
EMI Music Ltd.*

14. **Only Love** (3:20)
(Cosma/Gimble)
MCA Music*

15. **Any Dream** (2:42)
(Webber/Rice)
Webber/Rice/Novello & Co Ltd.*

* By permission

Total Time: 48:03

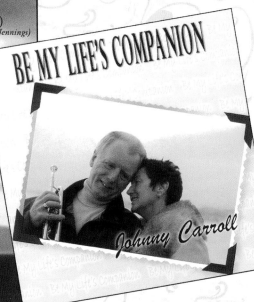

THE VILLAGE OF ROSES

The widely known "Glasson Carnival" the Midlands greatest centre of Entertainment takes place again this year in the Village of Roses. A Carnival known so well for its engagement of top Class Showbands and this year is no exception with Ireland's best, playing in The Goldsmith Country situated on the the shores of Lough Ree.

Glasson Carnivals magnificent Multi-coloured lighting system and decorations will again be in operation and more important to dancers its expertly laid maple floor. The Committee have decided to provide more dancing space and for the first time provide over 5,000 sq. ft of dancing space.

Most of our bands have played at Glasson Carnival from time to time with the exception of The Johnny Flynn Showband who recently topped the Irish Charts, other newcomers are The Kings from Naas and all the way from Derry The Emperors and The Woodchoppers who close our Dancing Programme.

We have our usual Senior & Junior football tournaments for Suir Valley and Mac Vita Cups between leading teams from Westmeath, Offaly and Longford, these tournaments proved to be a big success & attraction to followers of the game.

Glasson Carnival provide a free Car Park adjoining Marquee and First Class Entertainment for all patrons in The Village of Roses.

CEAD MILE FAILTE

SOUVENIR PROGRAMME

GOLDSMITH COUNTRY
1966

GLASSON

ATHLONE

FRIDAY
JULY 1st.

CARNIVAL

SUNDAY
JULY 24th.

(3 WEEKS)

DANCING
SUNDAY WEDNESDAY and FRIDAY
EACH WEEK

Ireland's Leading Bands Engaged

JUNIOR & SENIOR FOOTBALL

Souvenir Programme from 1966

139

DANCING PROGRAMME — ALL DANCES 9-2

GRAND OPENING DANCE

FRIDAY JULY 1st. Hueston Wells & The **PREMIER ACES**

SUNDAY JULY 3rd. **THE MIGHTY RHYTHM STARS**

WED. JULY 6th. Joe Dolan & THE DRIFTERS

FRIDAY JULY 8th. The Gallowglass Ceili & Modern Band

SUNDAY JULY 10th. *The Hi-Lows Showband*

WED. JULY 13th. Larry Cunningham & The Mighty Avons

FRIDAY JULY 15th. The Johnny Flynn Showband

SUNDAY JULY 17th. *The Emperors*

WED. JULY 20th. Richard Fitzgerald & His Ceili Band

FRIDAY JULY 22nd. *The Kings*   Final of Old Time Waltz Competition

CLOSING DANCE

SUNDAY JULY 24th. **THE WOODCHOPPERS**

BUSES EACH NIGHT FROM ATHLONE.   BALLYMAHON SUNDAY NIGHTS ONLY

Memories

140

*Relaxing before
a show*

*This one is
just for you*